Science Biographies

George Washington Carver

Ellen Labrecque

Raintree

Chicago, Illinois

Edited by Dan Nunn, Adam Miller, and
    Diyan Leake
Designed by Cynthia Akiyoshi
Picture research by Hannah Taylor and Tracy Cummins
Production by Helen McCreath
Originated by Capstone Global Library Ltd
Printed and bound in China by CTPS

17 16 15 14 13
10 9 8 7 6 5 4 3 2 1

Library of Congress Cataloging-in-Publication Data
Labrecque, Ellen, author.
    George Washington Carver / Ellen Labrecque.
        pages cm.—(Science biographies)
    Summary: "This book traces the life of George Washington
Carver, from his early childhood and education through his
sources of inspiration and challenges faced, early successes,
and the agricultural discoveries for which he is best known. A
timeline at the end of the book summarizes key milestones and
achievements of Carver's life."—Provided by publisher.
    Includes bibliographical references and index.
    ISBN 978-1-4109-6240-9 (hb)—ISBN 978-1-4109-6247-8 (pb) 1.
Carver, George Washington, 1864?-1943—Juvenile literature.
2. Tuskegee Institute—History—Juvenile literature. 3. African
American agriculturists—Biography—Juvenile literature. 4.
Agriculturists—United States—Biography—Juvenile literature.
I. Title.
    S417.C3L33 2014 630.92—dc23
2013014221

Acknowledgments
The author and publisher are grateful to the following for
permission to reproduce copyright material: AP Photo p. 27
bottom (The Ledger-Enquirer, Joe Paull); Art Resources
p. 23 (National Portrait Gallery, Smithsonian Institution);
Corbis pp. 9 (© Bettmann), 10 (© Corbis), 14 (© Corbis), 18
(© Corbis), 20 (© Bettmann), 22 (© Bettmann), 25 (© Hulton-
Deutsch); Getty Images pp. 11 (Photoquest), 28 (Archive
Photos); Iowa State University Library p. 12 (Special Collections
Department); Library of Congress Prints and Photographs
Division pp. 13, 15; Courtesy National Park Service, Museum
Management pp. 19, 24; NPS pp. 16 (George Washington
Carver National Monument), 26 (George Washington
Carver National Monument; Photo Researchers p. 5 (Science
Source); Shutterstock p. 27 top (© catwalker), design elements
(© SeanPavonePhoto, © Pablo H. Caridad, © Vasilius,
© Elena Larina, © sevenke, © Stockagogo, Craig Barhorst,
© sunsetman, © viphotos, © vadim.ivanchin); The Tuskegee
University Archives (Tuskegee University) pp. 6, 7, 8, 17, 21
(123456789/771); USDAgov p. 4 (National Archives and Records
Administration.

Cover photographs of George Washington Carver reproduced
with permission of Superstock (Culver Pictures, Inc.) and of
a soybean field reproduced with permission of Shutterstock
(© Fotokostic).

Every effort has been made to contact copyright holders of
any material reproduced in this book. Any omissions will
be rectified in subsequent printings if notice is given to the
publisher.

All the Internet addresses (URLs) given in this book were valid
at the time of going to press. However, due to the dynamic
nature of the Internet, some addresses may have changed, or
sites may have changed or ceased to exist since publication.
While the author and publisher regret any inconvenience this
may cause readers, no responsibility for any such changes can
be accepted by either the author or the publisher.

Contents

Some words are shown in **bold**, like this. You can find out what they mean by looking in the glossary.

Who Was George Washington Carver?

How many things can be made from peanuts? Ten? Twenty? Thirty? Not even close! George Washington Carver invented more than 300 ways to use peanuts, including making candy, milk, coffee, laundry soap, and hand lotion.

Carver spent his life inventing new uses for many crops.

Who was this great inventor? Carver was a man born into **slavery** who became a world-famous scientist in the field of **agriculture**. In addition to peanuts, he also worked with sweet potatoes and pecans. He spent much of his life teaching poor southern farmers new farming methods that helped them produce more and better crops.

HELPING OTHERS

Carver was a deeply religious man and never worked in search of fame or money. Instead, he worked for the joy of teaching and learning. He loved the wonders of nature and all the new things that can be made from plants.

"It is simply service that measures success," he famously said. He believed helping others in life was the most important thing of all. Carver devoted his life and work to doing just that.

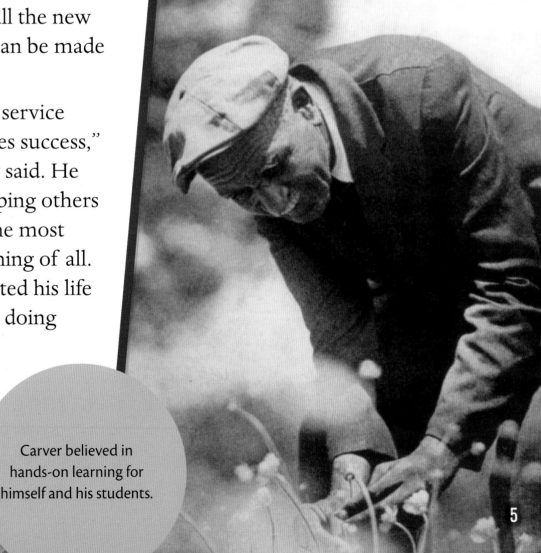

Carver believed in hands-on learning for himself and his students.

Born into Slavery

George Washington Carver was born into slavery in Diamond Grove, Missouri, in 1864. He lived on a farm owned by Susan and Moses Carver. George's father, Giles, was a slave who lived nearby. He died in an accident before George was born. Thieves stole George from the Carver farm when he was just weeks old, along with his sister and mother. Moses Carver reclaimed George, but George's mother and sister were gone forever.

This is Moses Carver, who brought George up after slavery was abolished.

The United States in Carver's day

George Washington Carver was born in the United States during the Civil War. The war was fought between the North and the South from 1861 to 1865. One of the reasons for the war was slavery. The northern states wanted to free the slaves, but the southern states did not. At the end of the war, slavery was **abolished**.

"THE PLANT DOCTOR"

The Carvers took in George, along with his older brother, Jim. George suffered from an illness called whooping cough throughout his childhood. He was not strong enough to help with farming. Instead, he filled his days wandering outside and being taught to read and write by "Aunt Sue," as he called Susan Carver. George was a natural gardener and earned the nickname "the Plant Doctor." "I wanted to know every strange stone, flower, insect, bird, or beast," he later wrote about his early years.

This photograph shows George with his older brother Jim in the 1870s.

The Quest for an Education

As George got older, he wanted to learn more than Susan Carver could teach him. The local school was for white children only. So, at age 10, he traveled 8 miles (13 kilometers) to a nearby town to attend a school for African American children. He lived with a childless black couple, Andrew and Mariah Watkins, and helped them with chores while attending the local school. In two years, George learned everything he could from this school's teacher.

Even as a young man, George thirsted for a chance to learn.

"Whites only"

Jim Crow laws existed in the United States from 1876. The laws made it so white people and black people were **segregated**. They had to go to separate schools, use different restrooms, eat at different restaurants, and sit in different places in public transportation. Jim Crow laws finally ended by 1964.

ADVANCED EDUCATION

George moved to Kansas in search of a more advanced education, and he soon graduated from Minneapolis High School in 1885. After high school, George applied by mail and was accepted to Highland University in Kansas. But when he showed up to begin, an official told him harshly, "We take Indians here, but no **Negroes**."

Black and white people weren't even allowed to drink from the same fountains.

FOR COLORED ONLY

College at Last

Carver was disappointed when his college dreams did not come true. For the next few years, he lived on the Kansas frontier in a **sod house** as a **homesteader**. Although he enjoyed living off the land, the rough winters and dry springs soon proved to be too tough.

This is a typical sod house like the one Carver lived in.

In 1888, Carver traveled to Winterset, Iowa, and got a job as a cook in a hotel. He met a white couple, John and Helen Milholland, at his local church. The Milhollands were impressed with Carver's endless curiosity. They encouraged him to try for college again.

COLLEGE DEGREES

In 1890, Carver enrolled at Simpson College in Indianola, Iowa, for one year. He then went on to study at Iowa State College of Agricultural and Mechanic Arts. He was Iowa's first African American student. Carver graduated with a **bachelor's degree** in science in 1894 and with a **master's degree** in 1896. He paid for his education by teaching other students and doing people's laundry.

An artist

Carver was also a talented painter. He took painting classes during his year at Simpson College. He painted detailed pictures of the flowers and plants he collected.

Carver painted his whole life and even won awards for his work.

A Professor

Carver made a wonderful impression on his teachers in Iowa. One called him "their most brilliant student ever."

In 1894, Carver was offered a position as a professor at Iowa State and became its first African American **faculty member**. Carver became an expert on treating plant diseases. He soon became so good with plants that he became famous!

This is Carver's graduation picture from Iowa State in 1894.

An Important Invitation

In the spring of 1896, Carver received a letter from the most famous African American at the time, Booker T. Washington. Washington asked if Carver would head the **agricultural department**, teach courses, and do research at the Tuskegee Institute in Tuskegee, Alabama.

At the time, Tuskegee was a college for black students, most of them poor. Washington wanted Carver to teach the poor southerners how to plant and harvest crops. Carver accepted Washington's offer and in reply wrote, "It has always been the one great ideal of my life to be of the greatest good to the greatest of 'my people.'"

A great man

Booker T. Washington (1856–1915) was an educator, author, public speaker, and advisor to many presidents. He worked tirelessly to educate and help improve the lives of poor black people.

Booker T. Washington was president of Tuskegee for almost 35 years.

Welcome to Tuskegee

As Carver rode the train to Tuskegee, he was **horrified** by what he saw out his window. "The acres of nothing but cotton," he wrote. "Everything looked hungry: the land, the cotton, the cattle, and the people." Decades of planting only cotton in the South had sapped the land of its **fertility**. The people and the land were starving.

Carver knew that for farmers to survive, they had to grow many crops, and not just cotton, as shown here.

HELPING TUSKEGEE

Tuskegee's campus was in bad shape, too. Most of it was a swampland, and classes were held in shacks. Carver got to work immediately, helping the local farmers, teaching his students, and building his **laboratory**. No matter how hard Carver worked, he still awoke early every morning and took a walk through the woods. He said, "When other folk are still asleep, I hear God best and learn his plan."

This photograph shows Carver (bottom row, center) with the Tuskegee staff.

Plant more crops!

Carver's plan was to teach farmers about **crop rotation**. When different crops are planted and rotated each season, they give **nutrients** back to the soil and keep it healthy. Carver encouraged farmers to grow crops other than cotton, such as peanuts and sweet potatoes. Crop rotation also keeps insects away that feed on just one type of plant and destroy it.

Too Many Peanuts!

Carver was tireless about spreading his message of crop rotation to local farmers. He also asked farmers to bring samples of their soil to him. He would test it and tell them what nutrients were needed to make it healthy.

People came to hear Carver explain the importance of growing crops that were healthy to eat.

Carver also ran his own "Experiment Farming Station." He planted crops to see which ones would thrive in the Alabama soil. He and his students also built and drove a wagon that went around to farms. The wagon was loaded with displays and equipment to teach the farmers his methods.

SUCCESS!

Carver also passed out easy-to-read pamphlets called "Carver's Experimental Agriculture Bulletin." They helped the average person learn about food and farming. Carver's program was a success. People became healthier because they had more food and recipes to eat and try.

Carver now had a new problem. Farmers began to grow and produce more peanuts and sweet potatoes than people wanted to buy. He had to find even more uses for the farmers' new crops.

Carver tested how to best grow all kinds of crops, including corn, at his Experiment Station.

Reuse and recycle

Carver was a big believer in recycling everything— whether it was using cow and horse **manure** as **fertilizer**, or old bottles and glass as equipment for his laboratory. Carver thought nothing should go to waste.

The Inventor

Carver spent hours in his laboratory trying to discover more uses for peanuts and sweet potatoes. He also tested different ways of cooking sweet potatoes and came up with many different recipes. He worked with every part of peanut and sweet potato plants, from roots to vines to skin and shells. He discovered he could use the peanut shells to make paper and different colored dyes, from black to orange and yellow.

Carver thought of his laboratory as "God's little workshop."

Carver also used peanuts to make flour, cereals, and lotions. The news about his inventions and discoveries spread throughout the land. He soon earned the nicknames "the Peanut Man" and "the Wizard of Tuskegee."

Carver invented different types of lotions, oils, and creams in his lab.

The peanut butter debate

Did Carver invent peanut butter? Although many people say he did, peanuts were mashed into a paste hundreds of years before Carver's day. And, in 1884, a scientist named Marcellus Gilmore Edson **patented** peanut butter. Then, in 1885, John Harvey Kellogg patented a process of preparing "nut meal." Although Carver is credited for discovering over 300 uses for peanuts, he did not patent any of them. "God gave them to me," Carver said. "How can I sell them to anyone else?"

Advice for All

All around the world, people heard about Carver's research. In 1916, he was elected as a fellow of the Royal Society of Arts of London, England. This was one of the highest worldwide honors to receive.

Carver received fan mail from all over the world.

In 1918, President Woodrow Wilson invited Carver to the **White House**. While there, Carver met with different groups of bakers and scientists. He taught them about the different products that could be made from the sweet potato, especially bread.

Helping the Peanut Industry

In 1921, Carver spoke in front of a committee of the **House of Representatives**. He spoke as a representative of the U.S. peanut **industry**. Carver talked about all that could be made from peanuts. He was only supposed to speak for 10 minutes. But the committee was so taken by his products, they told him "his time was unlimited."

This photo was taken at Virginia Polytechnic Institute, where Carver was invited to speak in 1928.

What's a tariff?

When Carver spoke in front of the committee, he convinced the government to put a **tariff** on peanuts. This was a high tax on peanuts from other countries. This meant they could no longer be sold to buyers at a cheaper price than peanuts from the United States. The high tax protected American peanut growers from losing their business.

Never About Money

Carver was offered big sums of money to leave Tuskegee and work elsewhere. The famous inventor Thomas Edison even asked him to come and work in his laboratory in Menlo Park, New Jersey. Carver said no.

Henry Ford

Henry Ford was a famous businessman and founder of the Ford Motor Company. He also asked Carver to come work for him in the automotive business. Although Carver declined, the two men developed a friendship and working relationship at the end of Carver's life. Carver and Ford worked together experimenting with ways to make a rubber substitute from weeds as well as a fuel for cars other than gasoline.

Henry Ford donated money to Carver to do more research.

FREE ADVICE

Carver did speak across the country at different colleges and even at county fairs. But he never charged for his talks and services. "My interest is scientific and not financial," he said.

Throughout his life, Carver lived simply on his $1,500-a-year salary in Tuskegee. He never bought more than he needed. Instead, he spent his life helping the poor people of the South to become better farmers and live better lives.

Carver helped people from all walks of life.

The George Washington Carver Museum

By the 1930s, Carver's age and health were starting to slow him down. He donated his life savings from over 40 years of teaching at Tuskegee to open a **foundation**, the George Washington Carver Museum. Businessman Henry Ford (see page 22) also donated financial support to help create the museum.

The foundation's goal was to encourage agricultural research by creating **scholarships** that would help pay for school for students with an interest in science. Today, the museum houses many of Carver's paintings, inventions, and products, as well as many of his early research tools.

The equipment Carver used included steam heaters, a burner, and a scale.

Peanut oil

Franklin Delano Roosevelt, president of the United States from 1933 to 1945, was a longtime admirer of Carver. Roosevelt contracted **polio** and lost the use of both of his legs by age 39. Carver believed rubbing peanut oil on withered limbs could help them get better again. He even sent Roosevelt a bottle of his massage oil. Although the oil was never proven to have healing effects, Roosevelt and Carver did establish a polio rehabilitation center for black people in Tuskegee. In 1939, Roosevelt awarded Carver a medal for all he had done in the field of science.

The George Washington Carver National Monument

On January 5, 1943, George Washington Carver passed away at his beloved school, Tuskegee. He was close to 80 years old. He was later buried next to the man who had brought him there in the first place, Booker T. Washington. Just six months later, President Roosevelt made Carver's birthplace in Missouri a national monument.

Visitors walking on the nature trail at the monument can get a sense of the things that excited Carver as a young boy.

The monument was the first ever for an African American and the first to honor someone other than a president. "The world of science has lost one of its most **eminent** figures," Roosevelt said at the time of Carver's death. "His achievements in the arts and sciences were truly amazing."

Carver's name

Although George Washington Carver died many years ago, he lives on in many ways. Many schools and parks are named in his honor. His face has appeared on postage stamps and a 50-cent coin, and even a U.S. submarine was named after him. In 1946, President Harry S. Truman declared January 5 "George Washington Carver Day."

George Washington Carver

32 USA

1998

G.W. CARVER HIGH SCHOOL

This Carver High School was opened in 2012 in Columbus, Georgia.

A Man Like No Other

In many ways, George Washington Carver was a man before his time. He recycled before most people even knew what that word meant. He tried to find natural ways to garden and farm without using dangerous chemicals.

Most importantly, Carver stayed true to himself and his personal beliefs. The **epitaph** on his grave perhaps says it best: "He could have added fortune to fame, but caring for neither, he found happiness and honor in being helpful to the world."

Carver was the happiest in his lab, making people's lives better.

Timeline

1864 George Washington Carver is born in Diamond Grove, Missouri

1885 Graduates from Minneapolis High School in Minneapolis, Kansas

1890 Enrolls at Simpson College in Indianola, Iowa

1891 Transfers to Iowa State College of Agricultural and Mechanic Arts

1894 Graduates with a bachelor's degree in science from Iowa State and becomes a professor while studying for his master's degree

1896 Graduates with a master's degree in agriculture from Iowa State; arrives at the Tuskegee Institute to become the school's agricultural director on October 8

1906 Begins using his travel wagon to educate local farmers on May 24

1916 Is elected a fellow of the Royal Society of Arts in England

1921 Speaks in front of the U.S. House of Representatives as an expert on peanuts

1928 Is awarded an honorary degree—a doctor of science—from Simpson College

1937 A bronze bust of Carver is unveiled on Tuskegee's campus

1938 The Tuskegee Institute Trustee Board develops the George Washington Carver Museum

1939 Carver receives the Roosevelt Medal for Contributions to Southern Agriculture Honorary Membership

1941 Henry Ford dedicates the George Washington Carver Museum at the Tuskegee Institute on March 11

1943 Carver dies at the Tuskegee Institute on January 5. On July 14, the George Washington Carver National Monument is established, on the Missouri farm where Carver was born.

1990 Carver is inducted into the Inventors Hall of Fame

1998 George Washington Carver is featured on a U.S. postage stamp

Glossary

abolish put an end to

agricultural department section of a college or university that studies the science of farming

agriculture science concerned with raising crops and farming

bachelor's degree degree awarded by a four-year college or university

crop rotation practice of growing different crops in the same area to keep the soil healthy and to keep bugs away

eminent famous and respected

epitaph words written on a person's gravestone

faculty member educator who works at a college or university

fertility capability of producing crops and vegetation

fertilizer something that enriches the soil and helps plants grow

foundation organization set up to serve the common good

homesteader person who rents land from the government and lives off it. Homesteaders make their own shelter, grow their own food, and maybe even make their own clothes.

horrified surprised in a bad way

House of Representatives one of two houses of the U.S. Congress (the other is the Senate). Its major function is to pass national laws.

industry certain type of business where goods are made and money is exchanged for them

laboratory space filled with equipment to conduct scientific experiments

manure animal excrement (solid waste) used to fertilize land

master's degree degree awarded by a college or university for at least one year beyond the degree awarded for four years of study

negro person of a black race; the term can be offensive and hurtful

nutrient supply for the soil that provides for life, health, and growth

patent gain legal rights and credit for the invention of something

polio viral disease that attacks the central nervous system and can cause permanent loss of strength and movement, commonly in the legs

scholarship money used to pay for a student's education

segregate separate one group from another

slavery ownership of one person by another; it involves a person working for another person without payment or choice

sod house house made from the top layer of earth that includes grass, its roots, and the dirt clinging to it

tariff tax set by the government on products coming into a country

White House home of the president of the United States, located in Washington, D.C.

Find Out More

There is more information about George Washington Carver waiting to be discovered! Start with these books and web sites.

BOOKS

Bolden, Tonya. *George Washington Carver*. New York: Abrams Books for Young Readers, 2009.

Carey, Charles W. *George Washington Carver* (Journey to Freedom). Mankato, Minn.: Child's World, 2010.

Dunn, Joeming W. *George Washington Carver* (Bio-Graphics: Graphic Planet). Edina, Minn.: Magic Wagon, 2009.

INTERNET SITES

Facthound offers a safe, fun way to find Internet sites related to this book. All of the sites on Facthound have been researched by our staff.

Here's all you do:

Visit **www.facthound.com**

Type in this code: 9781410962409

Index